CHUCK CLOSE
UP CLOSE

JAN GREENBERG AND SANDRA JORDAN

A DK INK BOOK
DK PUBLISHING, INC.

For my daughter Jackie, who views the world with an artist's eye. — J.G.

For my sweet sister Samantha. — S.J.

Quotes are taken from the authors' interviews with Chuck Close except for the quote
from the artist on page 7, which appeared in an interview with Michael Kimmelman in
The New York Times, 1997, and on page 12, a quote from Leslie Rose,
which appeared in "Close Portraits" by Lisa Lyons and Martin Friedman.

DK
Ink

DK Publishing, Inc.
95 Madison Avenue, New York, New York 10016
Visit us on the World Wide Web at http://www.dk.com
Copyright © 1998 by Jan Greenberg and Sandra Jordan
Library of Congress Cataloging-in-Publication Data
Greenberg, Jan.
Chuck Close, up close / Jan Greenberg and Sandra Jordan.—1st ed.
p. cm.
Includes bibliographical references.
Summary: A biography of the revisionist artist who achieved prominence in the late 1960s
for enormous, photographically realistic, black and white portraits of himself and his friends.
ISBN 0-7894-2486-X
1. Close, Chuck, 1940- —Juvenile literature. 2. Portrait painters—United States—biography—Juvenile literature.
[1. Close, Chuck, 1940- . 2. Artists.] I. Jordan, Sandra (Sandra Jane Fairfax) II. Title.
ND1329.C54G74 1998 759.13—dc21 [B] 97-31076 CIP AC
The text of this book is set in 18 point Weiss.
Printed and bound in the United States of America.
First Edition, 1998
2 4 6 8 10 9 7 5 3 1

CONTENTS

CHAPTER ONE

Becoming an Artist

 Step into Chuck Close's studio. You find yourself in a long white room with a thirteen-foot-high ceiling. Except for the colorful paintings lining the wall, the space is bare. The floor is cement, painted gray. Light pours in through a skylight. The studio is stripped for action, a place where work is done. Two unmatched chairs wait for Chuck's interviewers. A big bear of a man with a gentle manner, the artist talks about his work in an open yet carefully considered way. After pointing out a recently completed portrait of his thirteen-year-old daughter, Maggie (Figure 2), he discusses his own childhood. "When I was eight, I took art lessons from a woman in the neighborhood. I learned to draw from nude models. It made me the envy of all my friends."

Do the people who knew Chuck Close when he was growing up in Tacoma, Washington, still remember him? If his teachers come across his name in the newspapers or art magazines, do they recognize this celebrated artist as the uncoordinated kid in their classes with the Coke-bottle eyeglasses and the expectant smile? They didn't think he'd amount to much, let alone become famous. "I was 'dumb,' a 'shirker,' 'lazy'; my 'mind wandered.' This was written on my report cards."

Today he realizes that his school problems were caused by serious learning disabilities, but he wasn't tested and diagnosed until his own children were in school. During his childhood, in the 1940s, most educators didn't know about LDs or dyslexia. A student who had Chuck's trouble reading, spelling, concentrating, or paying attention was labeled slow or just plain difficult.

He spent hours by himself, drawing. "When every kid on the block wanted to become a policeman or fireman, I wanted to be an artist. It was the first thing that I was good at, the first thing that really made me feel special. I had skills the other kids didn't have. Art saved my life."

Chuck's big present one Christmas was an artist's easel. Then he saw a wooden box of "Genuine Artist's Oil Paints" advertised in a Sears, Roebuck catalog. "I bugged my parents for weeks until they bought it for me. To this day I can smell that cheap linseed oil in those tubes of paint."

Close's father, a sheet-metal worker and inventor, made many of Chuck's toys. "World War Two was going on, and a lot of stuff wasn't available in stores. He built me a bicycle from scratch and a pedal-powered Jeep I could drive around. He made all my model railroad mountains and bridges, too."

When Chuck was eleven, his father died. "Before that, I'd never picked up a hammer. After he died, I became very handy." His mother had taught piano at home, but now she took a full-time sales job to support the family.

Figure 2.
Maggie,
1996.
30" x 21",
Oil on
canvas.

Figure 3. Chuck Close in his New York studio painting Self-Portrait, *1991.*

"Why make art? Because I think there's a child's voice in every artist saying, 'I am here. I am somebody. I made this. Won't you look?' "

At school Chuck's learning disabilities made studying an ordeal. But instead of giving up he figured out his own way to concentrate. "I filled the bathtub to the brim with hot water. A board across the bathtub held my book. I would shine a spotlight on it. The rest of the bathroom was dark. Sitting in the hot water, I would read each page of the book five times out loud so I could hear it. If I stayed up half the night in the tub till my skin was wrinkled as a raisin, I could learn it. The next morning I could spit back just enough information to get by on the test."

Told by his school adviser not to bother with college preparatory classes, Close ended up at a junior college near his home after high school graduation. "The open enrollment policy meant anyone could sign up. Even someone like me who had never taken algebra, physics, or chemistry."

There he got lucky. The pride of the school was the art department. "The football team got new jerseys only if the art classes didn't need new supplies." Chuck had hoped to be an illustrator, designing magazine covers or cartooning for Disney, but after he took his first commercial art classes, he changed his mind. He would be a painter.

He went on to the University of Washington, and then this young man who had once been labeled "dumb" was accepted by the Yale University School of Art. The learning disorders had not disappeared. But the painstaking discipline he had

Figure 4. The artist's tools.

developed to get through school became the beginnings of a detailed system to organize his art.

"Almost every decision I've made as an artist is an outcome of my particular learning disorders. I'm overwhelmed by the whole. How do you make a big head? How do you make a nose? I'm not sure! But by breaking the image down into small units, I make each decision into a bite-size decision. I don't have to reinvent the wheel every day. It's an ongoing process. The system liberates and allows for intuition. And eventually I have a painting."

Figure 5. Eric, *1990 (in progress).* 100" x 84". *Oil on canvas.*

"I have trouble recognizing faces, particularly in three dimensions. I don't tend to recognize people on the street. But I do have a photographic memory for things that are flat. So by painting these large portraits and making them flat, I commit to my memory people who are important to me."

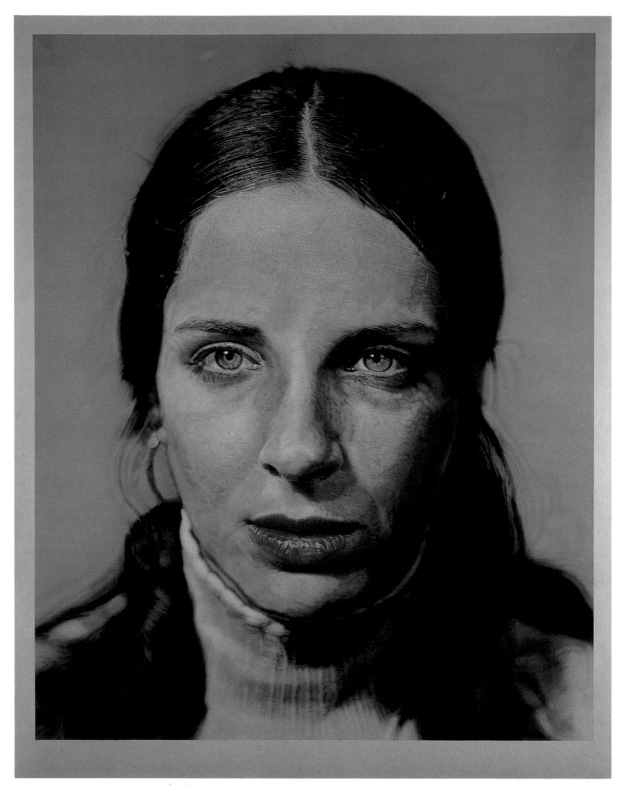

Figure 6. Leslie, 1973.
72 1/2" x 57".
*Watercolor on paper
mounted on canvas.*

Leslie says,
"Friends have had
awful reactions to
their photos. The
flip-flop left-right
reversal is one of
the reasons for the
shock. Chuck
often has stood
behind me and
looked past me in
the mirror, and we
sort of laugh at
each other. He
says, 'Is that what
you think you
look like?' "

CHAPTER TWO

"Sneaking Up on It"

 Chuck is talking with a group of art students in his SoHo studio. They ask how an artist chooses his subjects. What style to paint in? What color to use? He tells them: "If you formed a rock band, you'd know that you don't want to sound like this person or that person because you've spent thousands of hours listening to music. How can you decide what to paint without looking at thousands of paintings? There are no shortcuts. Every time I see a painting by somebody else it becomes part of the way I understand art. And I think, 'Wow! That's something I don't have to do.'"

Close's teachers always told him he had a "good hand." He explains this to mean both some technical ability and the knack of making "art that looks like art." In other words, he could paint in the traditional, accepted styles. "In college I made the same shapes and color combinations over and over again because I'd learned which ones looked most like 'art.' I was very good at mimicking other artists. In fact I couldn't get their work out of my head, particularly when I respected them."

Imitating other painters is part of learning to be an artist. But at some point

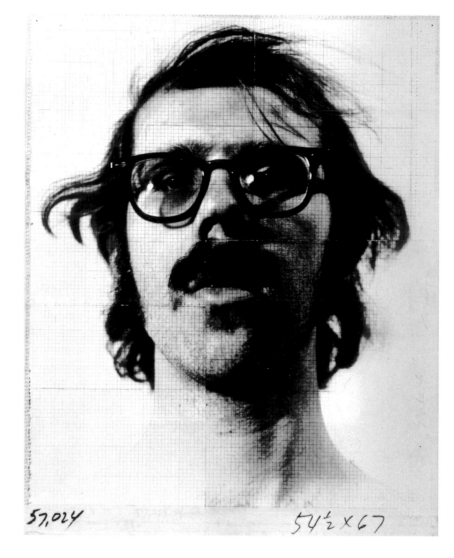

Figure 7. Self-Portrait maquette, 1968. Ink and felt tip on collaged photograph with masking tape.

The grid divides the photograph into many thousands of small squares. The artist translates the information for each of these squares onto the canvas.

57,024

54½×67

a serious artist develops his or her own style. For Chuck, this involved years of experimentation. After Yale he lived in Europe on a Fulbright grant. Then he came back to the United States and started teaching at the University of Massachussetts. "The first year I was an artist who taught. The second year I was a teacher who also painted. I wanted to be a painter. It was time to get on with it."

Chuck and his future wife, Leslie Rose (then a sculptor, now a landscape historian), decided to move to New York and get married. They set up a loft studio in SoHo, which at that time was still a run-down industrial area of the city. The loft had no heat and little hot water, but plenty of room to make art.

Chuck had gone through many different styles, including mixed media constructions made from cardboard, magazine photographs, and wedding pictures. But he needed to move forward, to "try something really drastic." To rid himself of his predictable painting habits, he threw away his familiar brushes and assembled a new set of tools: an airbrush, sponges, rags, and even an eraser stuck to the end of an electric drill.

He stretched a twenty-two-foot-long canvas. From photos he'd taken for a painting back in Massachusetts, he chose a full-length female figure. Close says, "Using photographs forced me to make shapes I'd never made before." But the results, while promising, missed several of his goals. He had attempted to make each part of the figure equally important, but there were too many areas to focus on. Some were naturally more compelling than others. In addition, the scale wasn't big enough. "I wanted the viewer to get lost in the painting." It wasn't practical to blow up the figure to a larger size when it was already twenty-two feet long. "What is the first feature most people look at when they meet someone?" he asked himself. The head. What about a giant head?

Figure 8. Big Self-Portrait, *1968.*
107 1/2" x 83 1/2".
Acrylic on canvas.

He happened to have some film left in his camera, so he stood in front of it and photographed himself. He stared straight into the lens as if he were taking a mug shot or a passport photo. The result was a photograph of himself looking like a hippie with an attitude—wild, stringy hair, dangling cigarette, and surly expression.

He divided the photograph into squares—a grid—and penciled in a matching grid on a seven-foot-by-nine-foot canvas. Then he translated onto the canvas each square of the photo, including the parts that were a little out of focus. With a razor blade he scratched the paint to get the hairs on his beard right, and he used the electric eraser to reproduce the reflections of light on his glasses.

Figure 9. Chuck, who is six-foot-three, stands beside Big Self-Portrait.

He made his painting as truthful as he could, even though the gigantic scale meant the imperfections of his face were magnified. He said he'd never considered the fact that his nostrils were shaped like lima beans, but in the four months it took him to paint the picture he had plenty of time to think about it.

Day by day he could tell the painting felt right. This was what he'd been looking for: a concept of self-imposed rules that would form the basis for future work.

What is revolutionary about this self-portrait? The large scale, the unsparing detail that forces the viewer to see the subject matter in a new way. The painting becomes a topographical map of a face with each freckle charted.

The familiarity of two eyes, a nose, a mouth, a chin is magnified into a question. Is this what we look like?

Between 1967 and 1970 Close painted seven more of the huge paintings. Their sheer aggressive size made them hard to ignore when they were first exhibited. But people were also amazed by Chuck's technique. His secret tool was the airbrush (a kind of sophisticated spray gun). "I used black paint that was thinned down, very watery. I scraped it. I erased it and sprayed more paint on. Slowly I sneaked up on it. In fact the whole series of black-and-white paintings was made with one sixty-cent tube of Mars black liquid paint."

Figure 10. Big Self-Portrait. *107 1/2" x 83 1/2". (detail) Acrylic on canvas.*

Gigantic. Smooth surface. Cool. Gray. Precise. Deadpan. Dazed. Quiet. Wordless. Every inch of the face is revealed. You can count the eyelashes. The pupils are larger than Ping-Pong balls.

In 1969 Close was invited to join an art gallery and to include his work in the Biennial of the Whitney Museum, probably the most prestigious group show for a young artist. In 1970 he had his first one-man show. Within five years his paintings were being exhibited from New York to Tokyo. The startling and original works had taken the art world by storm.

19

Figure 11.
Mark/Pastel,
1977-1978.
30 1/4" x 22".
Pastel on
watercolor-washed
paper.

CHAPTER THREE

Friends

Chuck Close is arranging to meet his friend the painter Mark Greenwold for lunch. "The restaurant is on Sixtieth Street. You can remember that because someday you'll be sixty."
He laughs as he gets off the phone. Mark, he says, has a terrible sense of direction and can never find where he is going. By the warm way Close speaks it is clear how much he likes his friend. In fact, he has done Mark's portrait more than twenty times.

Friends have always been important to Close. As a boy he was clumsy and hopeless at sports. "I couldn't catch a ball to save my soul. When I ran, I often fell down. So it was clear that if I was going to have any friends at all, I would have to find ways to get people to come to me and stay put." His father constructed a small puppet theater of wood and sheet metal in the backyard. His mother made a grand silk curtain for it "like the one at the Metropolitan Opera." There he put on magic acts and puppet shows. Soon his house became the center of activity for the neighborhood kids.

It is not surprising that years later, when he started painting from photographs, it seemed natural to choose his friends for models. "I didn't want to paint

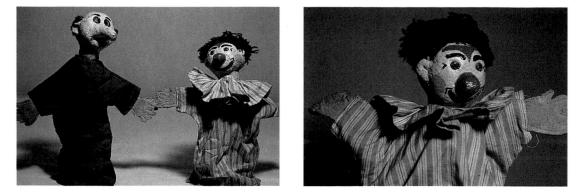

Figure 12a.
Hand puppets made
by young Chuck.

Figure 12b, below.
The artist, age 8,
dressed as a magician.
1948.

pictures of movie stars or famous people. I wasn't going to spend three to fifteen months painting someone I didn't care about." After his self-portrait, he made other big black-and-white paintings, including one of his good friend Philip Glass (Figure 13). The subject of the painting is now a well-known composer, but at

the time Close photographed him, Phil was just another member of their circle, a group of young, struggling avant-garde artists.

Close says, "I've recycled Phil Glass's image for thirty years, and it's produced thirty or more different pieces. Sometimes I think I should retire the photograph. Put it up in the rafters the way they do with basketball jerseys at Madison Square Garden." When he "recycles" the photograph, he changes the size or material. He applies different techniques

22

"I made puppets out of sawdust and glue."

and processes. For example, he has painted Phil in both large and small sizes. With an airbrush. With his fingerprints. With pulp paper. Reusing the same photograph has become a dominant feature of Close's work. "Some images I just connect with. It could be I'm especially close to the person or because it's an image that seems to matter more than others."

People often ask him what his friends think of their portraits. Mark Greenwold says he likes his, but after Close painted it, he grew a beard. Close says, "Almost everyone has some trouble dealing with these nine-foot-high images of themselves. It's difficult for people to accept how they look. Since the mid-1970s I've done all the photographs with a twenty-by-twenty-four-inch Polaroid so the subject is able to see his or her photo developing right on the spot. It's become a collaborative process. They all have strong feelings about how they present themselves."

Looking at these giant faces elicits strong reactions from viewers as well.

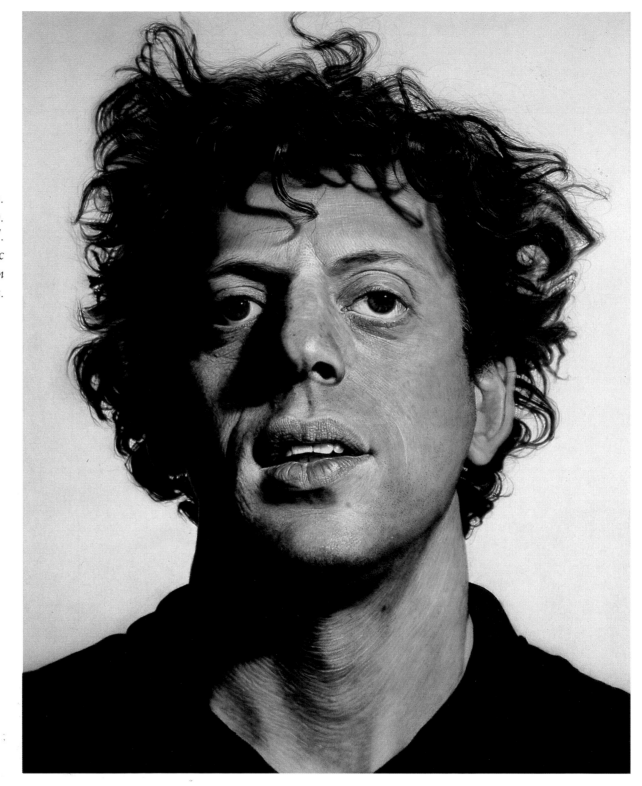

Figure 13.
Phil, *1969.*
108″ x 84″.
Synthetic polymer on canvas.

Our eyes move around the surface of a canvas like a bug crawling up and down, trying to find a place to hang on. What does the portrait tell us about Mark or Phil? Their faces stare at us coolly. Is the artist asking, "Do we ever really know someone, no matter how close we get to him?"

"Some images are more compelling than others. Sometimes for formal reasons. For instance, the way Phil's hair curls makes for a different outside edge with each new method of drawing."

Figure 14. Three images of Philip Glass in different media.

a. Phil II, *1982.*
64" x 53 1/2". Handmade gray paper, press dried.

b. Phil/Fingerprint II, *1978.*
29 3/4" x 22 1/4". Stamp pad ink and graphite on paper.

c. Phil/Watercolor, *1977.*
58" x 40". Watercolor on paper.

Figure 15. Chuck in his Bridgehampton, New York, studio painting Roy I, 1994. Finished painting is 102" x 84". Oil on canvas.

CHAPTER FOUR

"Putting Rocks in My Shoes"

It's summer. Chuck and his family have moved from New York City to a house/studio in Bridgehampton, New York. Even though he is surrounded by sea, sky, and rolling meadows, he is not tempted to paint a landscape. On the easel is a portrait of his friend the artist Roy Lichtenstein.

Close says, "The greatest enemy for an artist is ease . . . repeating yourself once you get good at it." To keep his painting from becoming too "easy," he sets obstacles for himself. He calls it "putting rocks in my shoes.

"I think problem-solving is highly overrated. Problem creation is much more interesting. If you want to react personally you have to move away from other people's ideas. You have to back yourself into your own corner where no one else's solutions apply and ask yourself to behave as an individual."

The giant black-and-white paintings had been strikingly fresh in the late 1960s. Now he was ready to create another "problem" for himself—a new challenge. Around 1970 he invited some friends over to pose for a different set of "head shots," this time in color. He says there is a big advantage to using

Figure 16. Five drawings from Linda/Eye *Series, 1977. Each 30" x 22 1/2". Watercolor on paper.*

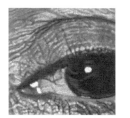  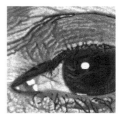  

a. Linda/Eye I—Magenta *(detail).*

b. Linda/Eye II—Cyan *(detail).*

c. Linda/Eye III—Magenta, Cyan *(detail).*

d. Linda/Eye IV—Yellow *(detail).*

e. Linda/Eye V—Magenta, Cyan, and Yellow *(detail).*

photographs. "If you paint from life, you have to do more than one sitting. The models gain weight, lose weight; their hair gets long; they cut it off. They're happy; they're sad. They're asleep or they're awake. But the camera provides the freshness and intimacy of one moment frozen in time."

To keep himself from making "the same old colors" on his palette, he found a way to mix the color directly on the canvas. Since color photo images are made up of three primary hues—red, blue, and yellow—he had the photographs separated into these three colors. Then he began to paint.

Figure 17. John, *1971-1972. 100" x 90". Acrylic on gessoed canvas.*
a. unpainted beard.
b. beard with red layer.
c. beard with red and blue layers.
d. beard with red, blue, and yellow layers.
e. finished painting.

The task was slow and painstaking. It took fourteen months to complete one picture because each one was painted three times, one color on top of another.

Moving around such large canvases proved backbreaking. So he built a portable desk and chair on the prongs of a forklift called Big Joe. By pulling on a rope, he could raise or lower himself to reach the whole canvas, from the bottom to the top. On

Figure 18. The artist, seated on Big Joe, painting Jud, *1987-1988.*

Big Joe were his paints, a television, a telephone, a radio. While he painted all day, he listened to news and talk shows. As he put the last touches on a painting, he turned on an Aretha Franklin tape to celebrate.

In another series Close made paintings without using brushes. His tools

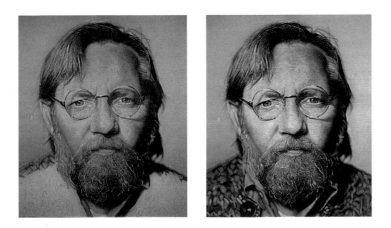

First the artist paints the red layer. Over the red he paints the same picture again, this time in blue. At last he paints the yellow layer. When these primary colors are mixed together in various degrees of intensity, they make up all the colors of the spectrum, from pinkish skin tones to midnight blue.

Figure 19. Georgia,
1984. 48″ x 38″.
Fingerpainting,
oil on canvas.

were his fingerprints, sometimes just his thumb rubbed in stamp-pad ink. "I like

using the body as a tool for painting. In a funny way you usually have to feel

through a brush, through a pencil. But there's this object between the body and

the surface of the canvas. By using my hands, I can feel just how much ink is on my finger, and then I can feel very clearly how much I'm depositing on the painting. This makes the ink easier to control." If you look at the background of this tender painting of his daughter Georgia (Figure 19), you can make out the artist's fingerprints in various colors.

Even though he was now painting in color, Close hadn't given up black and white. Fanny was painted in his familiar hyperrealistic way with every fold and wrinkle of her face visible, but instead of the airbrush he built the image out of broken chunks of fingerprints. The surface has become soft, feathery, and mysterious. The fingerprints look rubbed, not

Figure 20. Fanny, 1985. 102" x 84". Fingerpainting, oil on canvas.

"Fanny, my wife's grandmother, was a person who had tremendous tragedy in her life. She was the only survivor from her whole large family in World War Two. Given her experiences, it's amazing that she remained a very optimistic, lovely person. And both of those conditions are clearly present in her face."

crisp. From a distance you can't tell what method the artist used. Descriptive words that come to mind are wrinkled, gentle, warm, kind, weathered, and wise.

"I never intended to crank up the emotional content," Close says. "I found that if you present something straightforward, a person's face is a road map of his life."

Close's next great experiment involved thousands of vibrating dots of color. This time his aim was to "find a way that the colors would mix optically in your eye."

At three or four feet the individual dots of color that make up *Lucas II* are clear. They could be extra-large pixels on a color television or computer screen. If you prop up this open book and move away, your eyes will blend the dots. The confetti dots of crimson, green, azure, purple, and white merge into skin, hair, and eyes. With each step back the painting changes.

Now imagine walking into a gallery and being confronted by the actual painting of *Lucas II*. It is smaller than many of Close's heads—only three feet high—but its power dominates the room. His eyes drill into you. His hair crackles with electricity.

The starburst of color sucks you into a swirling vortex. Imagine a spaceship like the *Millennium Falcon* accelerating into hyperspace. On the other hand the painting also seems to radiate out, pulsing with an almost musical beat. Some descriptive words are speed, authority, explosion. If the head could talk, it would shout a command, not a polite request: "Do it now!" or "Follow me!"

Figure 21.
Lucas II.
1987.
16″ x 10″
Oil on
canvas.

Figure 22.
John, *1992*
(finished
painting, and
in progress,
right).
72″ x 60″.
Oil on canvas.

CHAPTER FIVE

"The Event"

Chuck is busy painting today. He's preparing for an exhibition and feels pressured. At the far end of the studio a tilted canvas rises out of a trapdoor in the floor. The Big Joe forklift has been retired. Now Chuck paints with a brush strapped to his arm. He works in this new way, dictated by what he matter-of-factly calls "the event," the event that changed his life.

"The event" happened in 1988, just before Christmas. Chuck was on the dais at the mayor's residence in New York City, facing a crowd of people. He was scheduled to give an art award but felt terrible, with a severe pain in his chest. He pleaded to be first on the program, quickly gave his speech, then staggered across

"I begin with one of the corners. After the squares are finished, I rotate the whole painting and go through it again. Finally the canvas is turned to its upright position. I go through the painting one more time, correcting, editing, changing, pulling one square out, putting one in. I'm always referring back to the photograph. It's like looking at a map so you don't get lost."

*Figure 23.
Richard, 1992. 72" x
60". Oil on canvas.*

*Figure 24. Lorna,
1995. 102" x 84".
Oil on canvas.*

the street to a hospital emergency room. Within a few hours he was paralyzed

from the neck down.

At first the doctors didn't know why. Eventually they diagnosed a rare spinal

artery collapse. Sometimes injuries like this happen to football players during

rough games or to people who have been in accidents. Nobody could figure out

how it happened to Chuck. But art and medical experts agreed on one point: His

career was finished.

Close knew better. He was alive, so he would continue to make art. But

becoming a conceptual artist, counting on others to execute his ideas, didn't

interest him. He yearned to get back to "the pure pleasure of pushing materials

around, of getting into paint." The biggest question in his mind was how. "I was trapped in a body that didn't work, but somehow I was going to get the paint on canvas."

His wife, Leslie, understood and was determined to find a way. She encouraged him to move to Rusk Institute, a rehabilitation facility. "I was there for seven months. Besides my family and friends, the art world also really turned out for me. At the end of the day after physical therapy, I'd be lying there, and one visitor after

Figure 25. Kiki, 1993. 100" x 84". Oil on canvas.

another would appear at the foot of my bed. In the darkened room their faces loomed up. I realized just how important these disembodied images of heads were. It reconnected me. It was the first time I ever really accepted the fact that I was making portraits. Prior to that I'd always referred to my paintings as heads."

He spent painful months in rehabilitation. Though he'd never worked out in a gym before, he went every day. Eventually he gained partial use of his arms and legs, but he could walk only a few steps. He'd be dependent on a wheelchair for

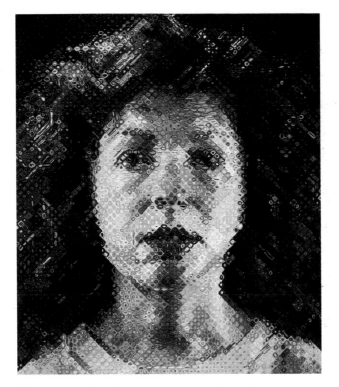

Figure 26a. April, *1990-1991. 100" x 84".*
Oil on canvas.

Figure 26b. April (*detail*).

the rest of his life. And even worse for an artist, he still couldn't move his hands.

He labored with weights, strengthening the muscles in his arms. Finally, after many long weeks of struggle, he developed a way to work. Seated in his wheelchair, with a brush strapped to his hand, he could put paint on a canvas. His arms took the place of his fingers.

"I used to like roughhousing on the grass with my kids, walking on the beach, or mowing the lawn. Since now there are so many activities I can't do, painting has assumed a larger share of my time. I'm really left with my relationship with my work, my family, my friends, and other artists."

Along with the complete change in his life, Close's portraits took on a new dimension. Before "the event" he was already painting in a looser, freer style, but now the shapes of each square were like fireworks—bursts of color. It was as if he were celebrating the sheer excitement of being able to paint again.

Step close to the canvas, and you see hundreds of little abstract paintings—multicolored ovals and gaudy squares, amoebas swimming before your eyes. Move back, and the portrait emerges. Perhaps first the mouth comes into focus, then the nose, the eyes, a full face beaming back at you.

A major leap! A triumph! A breakthrough, the critics would say. Close would simply say, "I was back to work."

Today Chuck Close is one of the most admired and successful artists in the world, with a hundred solo shows to his credit and a retrospective of his paintings at the Museum of Modern Art in New York City. How has he accomplished this? He says, "If you wait for inspiration, you'll never get anything done. When you look at my paintings, there is no way of knowing which days I was happy or which days I was sad, which days I was up or which days I was down. The important thing is getting into a rhythm and continuing it. It makes for a very positive experience. Every day when I roll out of the studio and look over my shoulder, I say, "That's what I did today."

Figure 27. Chuck Close's studio, with Self-Portrait, *1997.*

GLOSSARY

abstract—paintings in which the elements (color, shape, line, or texture), rather than a recognizable image, are stressed

acrylic—a type of fast-drying paint.

airbrush—a small, handheld machine for spraying liquid paint smoothly and evenly over a surface.

balance—refers to giving equal weight to the colors, shapes, lines, or textures in a painting.

brushstroke—the mark made by a paintbrush.

canvas—fabric on which the painter works. Usually it is stretched tightly over a wooden frame and nailed in place.

composition—the organization of the colors, lines, shapes, and colors in a painting.

cyan—the shade of blue used by printers.

elements of art—the basic parts of a painting: color, line, shape, and texture.

    color has three attributes: hue, intensity, and value. Hue means the six pure colors—red, orange, yellow, green, blue, and violet. Intensity refers to the brightness or dullness of a hue. Value refers to the lightness or darkness of a color.

    line refers to the mark the artist makes on the canvas. Lines outline a shape or connect one shape to another.

    shape and **form** refer to the appearance of a particular area in a painting, such as a circle, square, or triangle.

    texture refers to the surface of the canvas, especially the way it stimulates our sense of touch.

emphasis—a result of one part of a painting dominating other parts to capture the viewer's attention, such as the large heads in a portrait by Chuck Close.

grid—a network of evenly spaced squares.

magenta—the shade of red used by printers.

maquette—a work done by an artist in preparation for making a larger work.

medium—the material an artist works with; for example, oil paint, pencil, photographs, or pen-and-ink.

mixed media—an artist using several mediums in one artwork; for example, paint, photographs, and pen-and-ink.

model—a person who poses for an artist.

oil paint—slow-drying paint with an oil base that dries to a glossy surface.

Polaroids—instant photographs made with a Polaroid camera.

portrait—a painting of a person that is intended to give an impression of his or her character and appearance.

primary colors—red, yellow, and blue, or, in printing, magenta, yellow, and cyan.

proportion—the relationship of all the parts of a painting to one another and to the normal human figure.

rhythm—rhythm in a painting expresses movement by repeating colors, shapes, lines, or textures.

scale—size, either bigness or smallness, relative to the accepted normal size of a person, place, or thing.

self-portrait—a portrait of the artist made by himself or herself.

series—a group of artworks by an artist that are related by theme or subject matter or mediums.

spectrum—the range of color hues.

symmetry—the same on both sides. An even visual balance.

variety—refers to the way artists use the elements of art to provide contrast and visual interest in a painting, such as a variety of different shapes and colors.

What Is a Portrait?

Figure 28. Hans Holbein, Edward V of England, c.1538. 22 3/4" x 17 3/8". Oil on wood panel.

Over the centuries artists have painted portraits as a way of recording a person's likeness. The usual subjects were important people, such as kings, queens, religious leaders, and generals, who considered portraits part of their public images.

In this portrait of King Henry VIII's one-year-old son (Figure 28), the richly dressed baby has his hand raised as if he were bestowing a blessing. Holbein draws our attention to the painting's focal point, the prince's serious face, by the repetition of color around the canvas—the red velvety robe and hat, the crisp white cuffs and collar, and the curling white plume. The clothes and the Latin poem, which translates as "Little one imitate thy father and be heir of his virtue," are clues given by the artist to identify the status of his subject.

In colonial times in America portraiture was the most popular art form. Wealthy patrons preferred exact likeness to artistic inspiration. George Washington was sixty-four years old when Gilbert Stuart painted him. It is one of the best-known portraits in the United States, for reproductions hang

Figure 29. Gilbert Stuart, George Washington, 1796. 27" x 21 3/4". Oil on panel.

43

Figure 30. Pablo Picasso, The Artist's Daughter with a Boat, *February 4, 1938. 28 3/4" x 23 5/8". Oil on canvas.*

in many schools and public buildings. Washington's rosy complexion, the determined set of his mouth, the clear, steady gaze depict the first president of the United States as a firm, dignified leader. The vertical lines of the composition and dark, somber colors emphasize the artist's interpretation of Washington's character. What if Stuart had used bright colors with curving lines? What if the president had been grinning? How would the feeling expressed by the painting be different? Like many artists, Stuart was not in awe of his famous subject. According to him, Washington had just been fitted with a set of false teeth, which accounted for his stiff jawline.

The invention of photography in 1837 brought about a whole new attitude toward realistic paintings, especially portraits. Artists now were free of the demand to create a historical record of a person's appearance. The camera could do it more accurately. As a result paintings become more experimental.

One of the most versatile artists of the twentieth century was Pablo Picasso. In this portrait of his daughter Maya (Figure 30), her features are simplified, almost cartoonlike, painted in a variety of lively colors and shapes. The design is like a patchwork quilt. Even her face is divided into squares. With her legs thrust out stiffly, she resembles a toy doll. Picasso builds the composition on a series of geometric shapes. Is the feeling playful or sad? Does the portrait offer any clues that might help you recognize the real Maya?

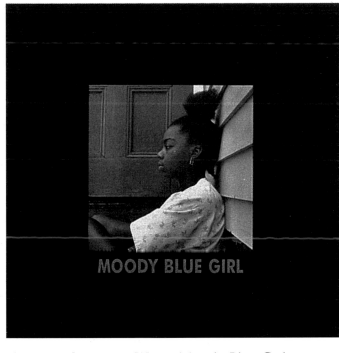

Figure 31. Carrie Mae Weems, Moody Blue Girl, 1997.
30" x 30". Monochrome color photograph, silk-screened
text on mat.

Figure 32. Georgia, 1982. 48" x 38". Pulp paper
collage on canvas.

For the photographer Carrie Mae Weems, making portraits is a way to represent what
has been underrepresented (Figure 31). Weems does not work with the sitter to take a formal photograph. She tries to capture people in unguarded, emotionally charged moments in
everyday settings. Her photographs are often displayed in a series that tells a story.

Compare Chuck Close's painting of his daughter Georgia (Figure 32) with the painting of Edward V by Holbein. The prince's regal look is very different from that of the casu-
ally dressed modern child. Which portrait is more realistic? Which way would you choose to
be painted?

LIST OF FIGURES

c. *Phil/Watercolor*, 1977. 58" x 40". Watercolor on paper. Mrs. Julius E. Davis Collection, Minneapolis.

Figure 15. Chuck in his Bridgehampton, New York, studio painting *Roy I*, 1994. Finished painting is 102" x 84". Oil on canvas. Subject is artist Roy Lichtenstein. Photograph by Ellen Page Wilson. Photograph courtesy of PaceWildenstein.

Figure 16. Five drawings from *Linda/Eye Series*, 1977. Each 30" x 22 1/2". Watercolor on paper. Oliver/Hoffman Family collection, Naperville, Illinois.
    a. *Linda/Eye I—Magenta* (detail).
    b. *Linda/Eye II—Cyan* (detail).
    c. *Linda/Eye III—Magenta, Cyan* (detail).
    d. *Linda/Eye IV—Yellow* (detail)
    e. *Linda/Eye V—Magenta, Cyan, and Yellow* (detail).
Photographs courtesy of PaceWildenstein.

Figure 17. *John*, 1971-1972. 100" x 90". Acrylic on gessoed canvas.
    a. unpainted beard.
    b. beard with red layer.
    c. beard with red and blue layers.
    d. beard with red, blue, and yellow layers.
    e. finished painting,
Subject is artist John Roy. Finished painting is in the Beatrice C. Mayer Collection, Chicago. Photograph courtesy of PaceWildenstein.

Figure 18. The artist, seated on Big Joe, painting *Jud*, 1987-1988. Subject is artist Jud Nelson. The finished painting is in the collection of Ron and Ann Pizzuti, Columbus, Ohio. Photograph courtesy of PaceWildenstein.

Figure 19. *Georgia*, 1984. 48" x 38". Fingerpainting, oil on canvas. Subject is a daughter of the artist. Hiroshima City Museum of Contemporary Art, Japan. Photograph courtesy of PaceWildenstein.

Figure 20. *Fanny*, 1985. 102" x 84". Fingerpainting, oil on canvas. Subject is Fanny Lieber. National Gallery of Art, Washington, D.C. Lila Acheson Wallace Fund. Photograph courtesy of PaceWildenstein.

Figure 21. *Lucas II*, 1987. 36" x 30". Oil on canvas. Subject is artist Lucas Samaras. Collection of John and Mary Shirley. Photograph courtesy of PaceWildenstein.

Figure 22. *John*, 1992 (Finished painting and photographs in progress). 72" x 60". Oil on canvas. Subject is artist John Chamberlain. Private collection. Photographs by Bill Jacobson. Photographs courtesy of PaceWildenstein.

Figure 23. *Richard*, 1992. 72" x 60". Oil on canvas. Subject is artist Richard Artschwager. Private collection. Photograph by Bill Jacobson, courtesy of PaceWildenstein.

Figure 24. *Lorna*, 1995. 102" x 84". Oil on canvas. Subject is artist Lorna Simpson. Photograph by Ellen Page Wilson, courtesy of PaceWildenstein.

Figure 25. *Kiki*, 1993. 100" x 84". Subject is artist Kiki Smith. Collection Walker Art Center, Minneapolis. Gift of Judy and Kenneth Dayton. Photograph by Ellen Page Wilson, courtesy of PaceWildenstein.

Figure 26a. *April*, 1990-1991. 100" x 84". Oil on canvas. Subject is artist April Gornik. The Eli and Edythe L. Broad Collection. Photograph by Bill Jacobson. Photograph courtesy of PaceWildenstein.

Figure 26b. *April* (detail). Photograph by Bill Jacobson. Photograph courtesy of PaceWildenstein.

Figure 27. Chuck Close's studio. On the easel is *Self-Portrait*, 1997. 102" x 84". Oil on canvas. Photograph by Ellen Page Wilson. Photograph by PaceWildenstein.

Figure 28. Hans Holbein, *Edward V of England*, c. 1538. 22 3/4" x 17 3/8". Oil on wood panel. National Gallery of Art, Washington, D.C. Mellon Collection.

Figure 29. Gilbert Stuart, *George Washington*, 1796. 27" x 21 3/4". Oil on panel. St. Louis Art Museum.

Figure 30. Pablo Picasso, *The Artist's Daughter with a Boat*, February 4, 1938. 28 3/4" x 23 5/8". Oil on canvas. Estate of Pablo Picasso/ARS New York. Photograph by Ellen Page Wilson. Photograph courtesy of PaceWildenstein.

Figure 31. Carrie Mae Weems, *Moody Blue Girl*, 1997. 30" x 30". Monochrome color photograph, silk-screened text on mat. Photograph courtesy of the artist.

Figure 32. *Georgia*, 1982. 48" x 38". Pulp paper collage on canvas. Subject is a daughter of the artist. Photograph by Maggie L. Kundtz. Photograph courtesy of PaceWildenstein.

BIBLIOGRAPHY

Books

Guare, John. *Chuck Close: Life and Work 1988–1995*. New York: Thames and Hudson, 1995

Lyons, Lisa, and Robert Storr. *Chuck Close*. New York: Rizzoli International Publications, 1987.

Catalogs from exhibitions and shows

Close, Chuck (Interview with Arnold Glimcher). "Chuck Close: Recent Work, February 21 to March 22, 1986." New York: The Pace Gallery, 1986.

Danto, Arthur. "Chuck Close: Recent Works." New York: The Pace Gallery, 1993.

Kertess, Klaus. "Chuck Close, New Paintings, September 23–October 22, 1988." New York: The Pace Gallery, 1988.

Lyons, Lisa, and Martin Friedman. "Close Portraits." Minneapolis: Walker Art Center, 1980.

Schjeldahl, Peter. "Chuck Close: Recent Paintings." New York: The Pace Gallery, 1991.

Articles

de Ferrari, Gabriella. "Close Encounters." *Mirabella*, November 1993.

Kimmelman, Michael. "Sought or Imposed, Limits Can Take Flight." *The New York Times*, July 25, 1997.

SOME MUSEUMS WHERE YOU WILL FIND WORK BY CHUCK CLOSE

Akron Art Institute, Ohio
Australian National Gallery, Canberra
Carnegie Institute, Pittsburgh, Pennsylvania
Des Moines Art Center, Iowa
Georgia Museum of Art, University of Georgia, Athens
The High Museum of Art, Atlanta, Georgia
Madison Art Center, Wisconsin
Milwaukee Art Museum, Wisconsin
Minneapolis Institute of Art, Minnesota
Museum of Art, Fort Lauderdale, Florida
Museum of Contemporary Art, Chicago, Illinois
Museum of Fine Arts, Boston, Massachusetts
National Gallery of Art, Washington, D.C.
National Gallery of Canada, Ottawa
Philadelphia Museum of Art, Pennsylvania
Princeton Art Museum, New Jersey
The Saatchi Collection, London
St. Louis Art Museum, Missouri
Seattle Art Museum, Washington
Toledo Museum, Ohio
Virginia Museum of Fine Arts, Richmond
Walker Art Center, Minneapolis, Minnesota
Whitney Museum of American Art, New York, New York
Yale University Art Gallery, New Haven, Connecticut

ACKNOWLEDGMENTS

Chuck Close was incredibly generous with his time, and we'd like to thank him for the thoughtful, gracious way he approached the project. Also we're indebted to Ronald Greenberg of Greenberg Van Doren Gallery and Arnold Glimcher of PaceWildenstein, who paved the way for us. Thank you also to Meg Duchovny of Grace Church School, and to our supportive friends Kathy Goodman, Donna Roberts, Nancy Arnold Goldstein, and David Gale. More thank yous to Andria Bundonis of PaceWildenstein, who spent hours with us locating prints and transparencies; to Michael Volonakis, Mr. Close's assistant, who patiently let us pester him with endless details and photographed the puppets for us; to our tireless and supportive agent, George Nicholson; and to the wonderful people who help us get from manuscript to bound book: our publisher and editor Neal Porter, art director Jennifer Browne, production whiz Barbara Greenberg, managing editor Laaren Brown, and publishing assistant Beth Sutinis.